100 Things

Every College Student With a
Disability Ought to Know

A self-orientation guide with definitions, customs, practices, procedures,
and advice to assist students with disabilities in adjusting to college.

by Kendra D. Johnson, Ed.D. and Trudie N. Hines

Cambridge Stratford Study Skills Institute
Williamsville, NY

100 Things Every College Student With a Disability Ought to Know

by Kendra D. Johnson, Ed.D. and Trudie N. Hines

Copyright © 2005
The Cambridge Stratford Study Skills Institute
A division of Cambridge Stratford, Ltd.
8560 Main Street, Williamsville, New York 14221

The
Cambridge-Stratford
Study Skills
Institute

Library of Congress Number: 2005921962
ISBN: 093563732X   Printed in the USA
Printing is the lowest number: 10 9 8 7 6 5 4 3 2 1

Introduction

Since 1990, the number of colleges, universities, community colleges, and vocational/technical institutions providing educational opportunities for students with disabilities has substantially increased. If you are one of those students, or are thinking of becoming a college student—Welcome! You have begun a journey filled with opportunity for personal growth and achievement. This book, *100 Things Every College Student With a Disability Ought to Know,* will arm you with information about how to make informed choices, how to receive accommodations for a disability, what type of assistance is available, and where and how to communicate your disability-related college needs.

Out of their conversations with countless college students with disabilities throughout the past ten years, the authors have summarized the crucial information students need to know to be successful in both academic and campus life. Student comments are included throughout the book, which is formatted for quick and easy reference.

The book includes seven chapters. The first, "Arriving," provides students with basic information about what to expect, think about, and do as they begin college. The second, "Paperwork," explains the typical information students may need to provide to request accommodations. The third, "Leveling the Playing Field," details the colleges' obligation to provide equal access for students with disabilities and discusses various accommodations. Chapter four, "The Classroom Experience," provides practical suggestions for productive and successful learning. The chapter covers campus customs, professor expectations and responsibilities, and class preparation strategies. Chapter five, "Campus Life," reminds students that college is more than academics, and chapter six, "Success Strategies," covers suggestions for success both in and out of the classroom. Finally, chapter seven, "Transitions: Moving On," provides helpful advice for moving from college to the working world or to further education. A suggested reading list and additional web resources are included.

100 Things Every College Student With a Disability Ought to Know is also a useful resource for high school students with disabilities who plan to attend college. It is equally helpful for school administrators, teachers, and parents who provide guidance and support for students with disabilities. We welcome your reactions, comments, and accounts of personal experiences as we prepare for our next edition. Please take a moment to complete the Editor Contribution Form found at the back of the book.

Best wishes for a great college experience,

Kendra and Trudie

Who Are The Authors?

Dr. Kendra Johnson is the Americans with Disabilities Act (ADA) Compliance Officer and Director of the Office of Accessibility at the University of Toledo. She has more than fifteen years' professional experience with issues pertaining to educational and workplace access for persons with disabilities. Dr. Johnson is also an adjunct lecturer in special education for the University's College of Education.

Trudie Hines has more than fifteen years' experience in higher education, including providing disability support services at both a selective public university and an open-door community college. She has also been an ADA compliance officer and has professional experience in student financial aid and scholarships. Ms. Hines is a Disability Services Specialist at Mott Community College in Flint, Michigan.

Collaboratively and individually, Kendra and Trudie have presented workshops at the local, regional, and national levels on the successful transition to postsecondary education for students with disabilities. They are frequent speakers at high school transition fairs for students with disabilities planning to attend – or thinking about attending – college.

Table of Contents

1 Arriving

Students With a Disability Ought to Know:

1.   that **college is an achievable goal** for students with the skill and determination. With the enactment of federal legislation preventing discrimination based on disability, students with disabilities are entering college at ever-increasing rates. Currently, one out of every 11 undergraduate college students report having a disability. *(National Center for Educational Statistics, 2002 http://www.nces.ed.gov/)*

Students With a Disability Ought to Know:

2.   that **entering or re-entering college is an adjustment for any student**. How quickly you adjust will depend on your preparation, personality, flexibility, and determination. All students feel apprehensive; you're not alone in facing this new experience.

Students With a Disability Ought to Know:

3.   that once you are admitted to a college or university, **the college wants you to succeed**. There is a substantial array of student support services for your benefit, such as writing assistance, tutoring, career and major exploration, and counseling services. Don't hesitate to take advantage of this free help.

Students With a Disability Ought to Know:

4.   that you are a **student with a disability—not a disabled student**. You will always be a person first; you should never be labeled by your disability. As in any walk of life, you may encounter people who are not familiar with the appropriate way to address you.   Feel comfortable with expressing your preference.

Students With a Disability Ought to Know:

5.   that a **disability, as defined by the Americans with Disabilities Act (ADA), is a permanent condition which substantially limits one or more major life activities**. Talk to the institution's Disability Support Services (DSS) office if you have questions about whether you might qualify for accommodations under the ADA. For more information about the ADA go to www.usdoj.gov/crt/ada.

CONGRESS AUTHORIZES THE ADDITION OF
FOUR NEW DISABILITY CATEGORIES TO
THE AMERICANS WITH DISABILITIES ACT.

Students With a Disability Ought to Know:

6.   that the **college admission application will not ask if you have a disability**. In fact, with limited exceptions, colleges are not allowed to ask you about your disabilities or your need for accommodations before you are admitted. But, you can choose to disclose your disability in a personal statement as part of the admission application. For example, you might choose to include something in your statement if you overcame challenges posed by a disability to achieve excellent grades or excel in community service activities. Keep in mind that admissions criteria will not be waived or lowered because you have a disability. However, highlighting your strengths as a student and what you have accomplished as opposed to your limitations may help you.

Students With a Disability Ought to Know:

7. that once you've been admitted, you will probably be asked to **come to an orientation**. Don't miss this chance to get important information about procedures, rules, college life, resources, and opportunities. Most orientation sessions will include a campus tour. Orientation sessions are also an excellent resource for making connections with fellow students. It's a good opportunity to make some new friends.

Students With a Disability Ought to Know:

8.   that if you will need **accommodations for an orientation**, including placement tests, provide advance notice. Some schools may need several weeks' notice to arrange for accommodations such as sign language interpreters or Braille materials. If you are blind or severely visually impaired, you need to schedule orientation and mobility training as soon as possible. There are often community agencies that will provide this service. The Disability Support Services (DSS) office should be able to provide you with information about available resources.

Students With a Disability Ought to Know:

9.   that in order to receive accommodations, **you are responsible for contacting the Disability Support Services (DSS) office**. In any educational setting after high school, you will need to identify your need for accommodations. Even if you received special education services in high school, the college is not aware of that fact.   The office may have a different name—like Accessibility Services, Office of Accessibility, Handicapped Student Resource Center, or similar—but there will be an office or person responsible for facilitating accommodations for students with disabilities. This office can be an important part of your academic career and a great resource, so get acquainted early on. Doing so as soon as possible will help you to fully engage in academic and college life.

"The Office of Accessibility is a great resource—use it." Brian, fresh-man, learning disability

Students With a Disability Ought to Know:

10. that **you should be prepared to answer questions about your disability and how it affects you in an academic setting.** You are the best source of information about your own preferences, strengths, and weaknesses. Be prepared for these questions and have your answers ready. You will feel much more comfortable with the entire college experience if you are at ease being your own advocate.

Students With a Disability Ought to Know:

11. that when you leave high school, the **Individuals with Disabilities Education Act (IDEA) does not apply to colleges and universities.** You will now be requesting and receiving accommodations under the Americans with Disabilities Act (ADA) and Section 504 of the 1973 Rehabilitation Act. The differences between the IDEA and the ADA and 504 are significant. It is to your advantage to become knowledgeable about those differences. For an overview, check out the chart at http://education.state.mn.us/mde/static/000196.pfd, or http://www.cgc.maricopa.edu/disability/pdf/acts.pdf. If you use a screen reader visit http://postitt.org//text/legal/compare.htm. You may be happy to have graduated from special education—just remember that you haven't "graduated" from your disability. You need to take an active role in knowing your rights, stating your needs, and finding and using accommodations.

"You have rights and don't let anyone stomp on them." Roberta, junior, ADD

Students With a Disability Ought to Know:

12. that if **you only recently became disabled or learned of your disability, you will need to familiarize yourself** with campus and community support resources. The DSS office can help you anticipate what accommodations you might need in an academic setting, but also check out community agencies pertaining to your disability.

Students With a Disability Ought to Know:

13. that **you should be familiar with support services you might need close to the college.** If you have a service animal, identify the local veterinarian; if you need medication, have a local pharmacy; if you may need counseling or psychiatric services, have an established relationship with, or referral to, local mental health providers; if you are a wheelchair user, know the closest source for service and consider bringing a back-up chair as a precaution.

Students With a Disability Ought to Know:

14. that you should know about the **vocational rehabilitation (VR) office** that serves your home area as well as the one serving the area where your college is located. If you qualify for services, this agency may be able to help you with the cost of special equipment as well as the cost of your education if college is essential to your employment goal. To identify the VR office in your vicinity, visit
www.jan.wvu.edu/SBSES/VOCREHAB.htm

Students With a Disability Ought to Know:

15. that **the real challenge is not getting into college, but successfully getting out.** This is true for all students. Take advantage of all the supports available—both on campus and in the community. Getting advice from students who have been there is often a great way to avoid pitfalls.

Chapter 1 Worksheet

Check each activity completed, and fill in the blanks with the information that may assist you as you begin your college journey.

_____   Admission application submitted   Date _____

_____   Acceptance received   Date _____

_____   Orientation scheduled   Date _____

_____   Accommodations for orientation requested Date _____

          Accommodations I requested are: _____

          _____

_____   Orientation/Mobility training scheduled
           (visually impaired or blind students)   Date _____

_____   DSS office contacted   Date _____

           DSS contact person's name _____

           Office location _____

           Phone number _____

_____   Meeting with the DSS office scheduled   Date _____

_____ Applied for educational assistance from the Vocational Rehabilitation Office

Location _____

Phone number/Fax _____

Contact _____

Important phone numbers:

Pharmacy _____   Doctor(s) _____

_____

Veterinarian _____   _____

Equipment supply/repair _____

2 Paperwork

Students With a Disability Ought to Know:

16. that you will need to provide **documentation of your disability** to the Disability Support Services (DSS) office. Each school may have slightly different standards for proper documentation, so you need to check their requirements. You only need to provide documentation if you are requesting accommodations. Documentation of any disability must be provided by an appropriate professional.

Students With a Disability Ought to Know:

17. that your documentation should include details about your **current limitations and how the disability will affect you in an academic setting.** This information helps the college identify, in collaboration with you, what accommodations will best meet your needs. Your experience adds valuable information to be considered with your documentation.

Students With a Disability Ought to Know:

18. that the **Family Educational Rights and Privacy Act (FERPA) limits the information the DSS office can share about you.** You may have to provide specific written permission to allow the DSS office to discuss your situation with others, including your parents. This includes information about your grades and academic progress. Generally, disability and academic information is kept confidential except for faculty or staff who have a legitimate academic interest or need to know. The DSS office may need to communicate limited information to effectively provide accommodations. For more information on FERPA, visit www.ed.gov/offices/OM/fpco/ferpa .

Students With a Disability Ought to Know:

19. that if you had an **Individualized Education Program (IEP) in high school,** a copy of the IEP may not be all you need to provide. Details of any testing done or additional medical information may be needed. IEPs do not apply to college. If you had a "504 Plan" in high school, check with the DSS office about your eligibility for services.

Students With a Disability Ought to Know:

20. that you can find examples of guidelines for **documenting learning disabilities** at www.ahead.org/, www.ets.org/ or www.act.org/. Many schools are using these suggested standards. Most colleges will ask for test results from within the past three to five years. Some may accept older information if the tests used were designed for adults.

Students With a Disability Ought to Know:

21. that you also can find examples of standards for **documenting ADD or ADHD** at <u>www.ahead.org/</u>, <u>www.ets.org/</u> or <u>www.act.org/</u>. A brief note on a physician's prescription pad stating that you have ADD or ADHD may not be accepted by some colleges. Be prepared to provide more detailed information.

Students With a Disability Ought to Know:

22. that you should check with the DSS office about guidelines for **documentation of other disabling conditions** such as psychiatric, vision, hearing, neurological, chronic health conditions, traumatic brain injuries, and acquired brain injuries. Even though you may have an obvious disability, information about your current limitations helps the college provide what you need.

Students With a Disability Ought to Know:

23. that colleges may have **different requirements for how recent the information needs to be**. You may need to provide more recent reports for conditions which can change in a short period of time. Some colleges will help you send for your most recent documentation by having you sign a release to have the diagnosing professional send the information to the DSS office. Students are strongly encouraged to obtain updated documentation before leaving high school.

Students With a Disability Ought to Know:

24. that **colleges and universities are not required to conduct or pay for an evaluation to document your disability.** However, the college or university has the right to request more information from you if what you provided is insufficient. Remember, adequate documentation is a critical factor in identifying what accommodations or other assistance you may be eligible to receive based on your disability.

Students With a Disability Ought to Know:

25. that **your transcripts will not show you received accommodations**. Information regarding your disability won't be included on your transcript or college degree. Information about your disability is kept separate from your academic records.

Students With a Disability Ought to Know:

26. that you should always **keep a copy of the documentation of your disability in your personal files.** There may be other times when you will need this documentation, such as when asking for accommodations in the workplace or requesting accommodations in graduate school.

Chapter 2 Worksheet

Requesting accommodations will require written verification of your disability from an appropriate professional. Understanding your disability documentation will assist you in being able to effectively self-advocate. Fill in the following information using your written documentation of disability.

_____ I know what the school requires for documentation of my disability.

_____ I have written documentation of my disability from a qualified professional.

My disability as defined in my documentation _____

_____

My documentation was prepared by: _____

      Title_____ Date _____ Phone _____

I can describe the current limitations caused by my disability as _____

_____

_____

In the classroom, this affects my ability to_____

_____

_____

How this affects my studying _____

_____

_____

In outside activities/work, this affects my ability to _____

_____

_____

_____I have submitted this documentation to the DSS office and have followed
their procedures for requesting accommodations based on that documentation.

3 Leveling the Playing Field

Students With a Disability Ought to Know:

27. that **accommodations are intended to level the playing field** by removing barriers so you have an equal opportunity to access the programs, activities, and services of the college. Accommodations will not alter the essential requirements of a course or the core curriculum of a program. Accommodations do not guarantee passing grades. Accommodations provide a fair chance for students who are otherwise qualified; they do not provide an unfair advantage.

"Don't expect anything to be handed to you. If you want it, work for it." Anonymous

Students With a Disability Ought to Know:

28. that **determining appropriate accommodations is an interactive process** between you, the DSS office, faculty or other relevant administrator. You should express your preferences, however, final determination is based on a number of factors. Remember, you are the primary player in the accommodation process. If you are older than 18, your parent(s), spouse, or other support person cannot initiate accommodation requests for you.

Students With a Disability Ought to Know:

29. that **students accustomed to special treatment in high school may be surprised by the absence of the same conditions on the college campus**. Aids provided to accommodate students with disabilities do not have to be the most sophisticated, but they must be effective for the individual student. As a result, in some instances students may not receive their preferred accommodation, but the one offered by the institution must provide equal access.

"Know what you need and don't be afraid to ask for it."   Cindy, *sophomore, blind*

Students With a Disability Ought to Know:

30. that you need to be **adaptable and flexible**. Identifying effective accommodations in new situations can require creativity and patience by everyone involved. By working collaboratively with the DSS staff, coming prepared with suggested accommodation strategies, and being willing to try accommodations you haven't used before, you may discover solutions more effective than you had previously experienced. The structure of a particular course and the circumstances of your disability may require brainstorming with the instructor to come up with creative ways to let you fully participate in the course and demonstrate what you have learned.

"The instructors for a video production course said I couldn't do it. After they told me why I couldn't, I told them how I could. And I got an A!" Jason, communication major, graduate, blind

Students With a Disability Ought to Know:

31. that **all accommodations are determined on an individual basis**. There is no general rule applied to everyone with the same disability; all students' accommodations are based on their documentation, their unique strengths and limitations, and the nature of the course or activity.

Students With a Disability Ought to Know:

32. that **you must disclose your disability to the DSS office to receive accommodations**. Disclosing a non-visible disability such as psychological, learning, or medical is a personal decision. When and how to disclose must be weighed carefully, but you should consider the benefits.

Students With a Disability Ought to Know:

33. that **examples of academic accommodations** may include in-class note takers, alternative format text materials, preferred seating, tape-recorded lectures, sign language interpreters, extended testing time, tests in a distraction-reduced location, readers or scribes for tests, assistive listening devices, and use of assistive devices or technology, among others. Accommodations provided for you are based on your unique needs.

Students With a Disability Ought to Know:

34. that **accommodations may vary from course to course**. Because the nature of courses may be very different (a lecture course vs. laboratory science course vs. field experience), your disability may present very different challenges in each. As a result, you may need accommodations in one course, but none in another. Your accommodations will be designed for each circumstance.

Students With a Disability Ought to Know:

35. that **advances in technology are constantly expanding the range of accommodations available** to students. What were once challenging communication issues can now be solved using technology. For example, voice recognition programs allow you to speak and the computer to type what you say; screen reading programs will read scanned material or text files; and sign language interpreting can be delivered from a remote site using video streaming technology. Check with the DSS office to see what's available on your campus.

Students With a Disability Ought to Know:

36. that if your **disability limits your access to printed text, technology now offers solutions that allow you to be more independent**. Scan and read programs, electronic text (e-text), and text-to-MP3 files are taking the place of books recorded on tape. With some basic computer equipment and software, these options allow you to have faster access to information without having to wait for someone to read the material. Recording for the Blind and Dyslexic, www.rfbd.org , offers some options for e-text. Kurzweil Educational Systems, www.kurzweiledu.com , offers a multi-faceted scan/read/ speech/study tools program, one of many software options available. You should learn to use adaptive technology before you come to campus. For example you can "try out" the scan/read program "Read Please" by going to their website at www.readplease.com/ .

Students With a Disability Ought to Know:

37. that if **you need a reader or a scribe, these may be provided for tests or in-class work, but not for routine assignments outside of class or research projects.** You need to have a way to accomplish these tasks. Technology may provide you with solutions. Check out resources at sites such as The Alliance for Technology Access www.ataccess.org or ABLEDATA www.abledata.com .

Students With a Disability Ought to Know:

38. that **accommodations would be considered unreasonable** if they fundamentally alter the essential elements of an academic program, curriculum or course, or lower the standards; threaten the health or safety of yourself or others; or cause undue financial hardship for the institution. Most accommodations identified will be readily achievable, though there may be less flexibility when degree requirements lead to certifications or licenses, such as fields associated with medicine.

Students With a Disability Ought to Know:

39. that **you cannot be charged a fee for accommodations**. The college will bear the cost of accommodations provided. In some cases, another agency may contribute to the cost of accommodations, but it is the college's responsibility to ensure they are provided to you at no cost.

Students With a Disability Ought to Know:

40. that there is a **difference between accommodations and personal services**. Services are generally more personal in nature—like personal care attendants, tutors, mobility assistance, transportation, readers for homework assignments, and study coaches. Colleges are required to provide accommodations, but not personal services. If needed, you should arrange for personal services before the start of the semester so you will not miss any classes or assignment deadlines. Check with your local Center for Independent Living (CIL) for assistance. To find the CIL nearest you visit http://www.bcm.tmc.edu/ilru/jump1.htm.

Students With a Disability Ought to Know:

41. that **students with disabilities have access to tutors on the same basis as other students.** Although tutoring is considered a personal service, not an accommodation, the good news is that some tutoring is available on many campuses. Don't hesitate to use the tutoring help available and don't hesitate to ask if the tutors have been trained in working with students with disabilities. Many of the best students use tutors.

Students With a Disability Ought to Know:

42. that **professional tutors or learning specialist tutors may be available at some colleges.** There may be a charge for these services because they are not required to be provided. Many colleges and universities have programs that go beyond the minimum requirements of the ADA, and provide specialized services for your disability needs. The Peterson's publication, *Colleges with Programs for Students with Learning Disabilities or ADD,* may help you find the type of program that best meets your needs.

Students With a Disability Ought to Know:

43. that you should **take advantage of the accommodations and services available**. It is best to use them rather than try to do without and find out you could have done better. You most likely will not be allowed to redo work if you were offered an accommodation and chose not to use it.

"I was too embarrassed to use accommodations until I started flunking. Use what they offer you to be successful." Melissa, senior, psychological

Students With a Disability Ought to Know:

44. that you should **identify the ADA Coordinator for your institution**. While the DSS office is responsible for the administration and delivery of direct services and accommodations to students with disabilities, the ADA Coordinator is responsible for management of institution-wide compliance activity. Complaints regarding non-compliance with disability legislation may be directed to the ADA Coordinator. The DSS office should be able to provide you with the name and contact information of the ADA Coordinator at your institution.

Students With a Disability Ought to Know:

45. that **colleges and universities are required to adopt procedures for students to file a disability grievance or complaint**. Contact your DSS office or the ADA Coordinator to review existing policies on your campus. Students who have not been successful in resolving a disability-related complaint internally can contact the U.S. Department of Education Office of Civil Rights (OCR). To learn more about the OCR complaint process, visit the OCR website at www.ed.gov/ocr/docs/howto.html.

Students With a Disability Ought to Know:

46. that **while most colleges and universities do what is necessary to meet the minimum requirements of the law, many will exceed those requirements—focusing instead on the "spirit" of the law**. Do your homework when investigating the institutional climate at your school toward students with disabilities. The culture of acceptance and the value placed on diversity will vary from campus to campus.

Chapter 3 Worksheet

Thinking about and completing the following information will be helpful as you discuss possible effective academic accommodations with the DSS office.

My academic strengths are _____

_____

_____

I have the most trouble with_____

_____

_____

I learn best by (i.e. hearing, seeing, doing, etc.) _____

_____

I take good notes.   Yes ❑   No ❑

I have good computer skills.   Yes ❑   No ❑

I know how to use assistive technology
which addresses some of my limitations.   Yes ❑   No ❑

The technology I know how to use (including software) is _____

_____

_____

Accommodations (modifications/support) I plan to ask for in college _____

_____

_____

Review your documentation and complete the following:

The above accommodations can be directly related
to the diagnosis in my written documentation.   Yes ❑   No ❑

        If no, my plan to update documentation _____

_____

4 The Classroom Experience

Students With a Disability Ought to Know:

47.   that the **first semester will generally be the toughest for any student**. It may be even more so for students with disabilities because the first semester is often a testing period for identifying the accommodations that will best meet your needs. Balancing your course load with your disability is essential to your success. You may want to take fewer credits—especially the first semester—until you find a comfortable level for your abilities and time requirements.

"Don't take a full load your first semester. I did, despite advice not to, and failed most of my courses." R.C., sophomore, learning disability

Students With a Disability Ought to Know:

48.   that **you need to do a reality check when choosing your course of study or major**. Do an honest assessment of your strengths and weaknesses, your abilities and limitations, and the requirements of the specialty or profession. Consider what assistive devices or technology might be available, and if reasonable accommodations will allow you to meet the requirements. Hopefully your disability will not be a barrier to reaching your educational goal as long as you know what program is the best match for you.

Students With a Disability Ought to Know:

49.   that **some programs have developed technical standards which students must meet.** For example, programs such as physical therapy may require students to have the ability to lift a minimum weight. Talk with the program staff or faculty if you have concerns before you get into the program.

Students With a Disability Ought to Know:

50.   that **the 3 Rs (basic skills)** we always heard about are still needed for college work: reading, (w)riting, and 'rithmetic. No accommodation will make up for lack of academic preparation. If your placement tests show you have deficiencies in any of these areas, take developmental coursework offered at your institution or a community college before tackling higher-level courses. If you are at a four-year institution, check with your advisor to see if the credits will transfer back to your institution.

"I got by in high school without doing very much work and still made fairly good grades—but not in college. I found that I was unprepared, and accommodations didn't make the difference." Chris, senior, learning disability

Students With a Disability Ought to Know:

51. that you need to **choose your program and classes with a realistic understanding of your reading and comprehension levels.** College textbooks are written at the 12-13th grade level. Choose your major and your classes with this in mind. You don't want to take a reading improvement class at the same time as a course that requires heavy reading from an advanced-level text.

"Don't try to do everything your freshmen year or you will get overwhelmed. Take a light course load at first." Jonathan, junior, mobility impaired

Students With a Disability Ought to Know:

52.   that **you need to balance the requirements of the course with the impact of your disability.** If you have a disability that makes it difficult to access or comprehend text, don't fill your schedule with courses that all have large reading assignments. If you have a mobility impairment, allow yourself sufficient time to travel between classes. Advisors, counselors, and DSS staff can help you make good choices.

"Pick an early registration date so all the classes won't be gone."
Sakib, freshman, learning disability

Students With a Disability Ought to Know:

53.   how your disability affects your learning. If you have a traumatic brain injury (TBI), know what processing deficits you may have. If you use medication for a psychological disability, understand its effects on your mental processing. An in-depth understanding of how your disability impacts you will assist in the identification of classroom accommodations that will best meet your needs.

Students With a Disability Ought to Know:

54. that **if you have a learning disability in the area of math, the longer you wait to take math, the less you may remember**. For some students, taking their math course the first semester while simultaneously learning math study skills may result in a higher success rate. An alternative is to brush up your math skills with a tutor during one semester and immediately take your math course the next. For an excellent source for math study skills tools, visit www.academicsuccess.com.

Students With a Disability Ought to Know:

55.   that **checking out the syllabus for each course** may help you decide if this course is right for you this semester. Most courses will have a syllabus which will outline the required texts, assignments, timeline, number of exams, writing and research assignments, and attendance and grading policies. This information can be essential for planning your schedule and needs, and for planning accommodations.

Students With a Disability Ought to Know:

56. that **there is no special ed. in college**. You will be in the same classes as all other students, must do the same amount of work, and will be scored on the same scale.   Depending on the school, you could be in a large auditorium with a hundred other students, or in a class of ten.

Students With a Disability Ought to Know:

57.   that you need to **do some research before choosing instructors.** Try to find the instructors who are experienced at accommodating, who use a variety of teaching methods—who aren't just talking heads in front of the room—and who have a good relationship with the DSS office. Sometimes the best source for information about instructors is other students, especially students with disabilities.

CRAZY LIKE A FOX

Students With a Disability Ought to Know:

58.   that some colleges offer **priority or early registration** to students with certain disabilities. This means that the DSS office will be able to arrange to get you registered in classes before other students register, or at least early in the registration period. This will help you get into the classes you need before they are filled. This may be important if you have to depend on special transportation, or need to attend during certain hours because of a medical condition.

"You don't have to have an obvious disability to receive help. I never knew that because of my diabetes I could take advantage of priority registration or that it even existed. If you are having difficulties—just ask and someone will eventually point you in the right direction." Lisa, graduate, chronic health

Students With a Disability Ought to Know:

59.   that many DSS offices will provide you with **a written document, generally known as an advocacy memo, that spells out the kinds of accommodations that they think might work for you.** You will likely need to bring that memo to your instructors. Meet with your instructors during their office hours at the beginning of the semester. This will be a chance to give him/her the explanation memo from the DSS office and to discuss your accommodation needs. Having this meeting will also avoid uncomfortable conversations in front of the class. Although professors typically follow the recommendations made by the DSS office, individual course outcomes and professors' expectations vary and some negotiation of accommodations may very well be necessary.

"I appreciate students coming in during office hours to discuss accommodations. It lets me know who they are, and I can spend time understanding what they are requesting." Prof. Bradley Whittaker, English

Students With a Disability Ought to Know:

60.   that you should **check out your classrooms before classes begin**. This is especially important if you will need special seating arrangements because of a service animal, have adjustment issues and need to become familiar with your surroundings, need to be located near electrical outlets, or need a certain type of chair or writing surface. Allow enough time for the college to make changes or move furniture before classes start.

Students With a Disability Ought to Know:

61.   that **if you have mobility impairments, the classroom needs to be accessible and be located in an accessible building**. Locate your paths of travel, accessible entrances, and seating arrangements in the classroom.   Schools have a responsibility to move a classroom if it is inaccessible.

Students With a Disability Ought to Know:

62.   that you need to **check with the DSS office before the beginning of the semester** to discuss any special requirements you may have for your classes. If you will need alternative format texts, it is common for schools to require one to two months' lead time. Plan accordingly. Likewise, if you will need sign language interpreters, C-Print, TypeWell or real-time captioning, you may also be required to provide more advance notice than for other accommodations.

Students With a Disability Ought to Know:

63.   that you should also **check with your professors two to three weeks before the start of the semester to identify any particular circumstances that will require advance planning**. In-class writing assignments, field trips, pop-quizzes, and lab work are some examples of course activities that may require accommodations in the classroom. Waiting to discover these things the first day of class can put you at a disadvantage.

Students With a Disability Ought to Know:

64.   that you should **request permission from instructors to audio-tape lectures if you have difficulty taking notes**. Most instructors will not mind, and it is often customary for students with and without disabilities to record lectures. However, because of intellectual property concerns, advance permission may be required by some instructors. Don't hesitate to ask for assistance from the DSS office if you encounter difficulty gaining the instructor's permission.

Students With a Disability Ought to Know:

65. that **some classes have attendance requirements**, especially those that require in-class projects or group interaction. If your disability may cause you to occasionally or frequently miss class, you may want to consider an alternative choice. Note takers cannot take the place of classroom participation.

Students With a Disability Ought to Know:

66.   that if you have a **speech impediment which may cause difficulty communicating** in some settings, speak with your professor and develop a plan, especially if class discussions or oral presentations are required. Students who are deaf or hard of hearing should consider how they want to handle class presentations in advance. Oral presentations can be signed, but this requires coordination with an interpreter. Knowing how you can deal with classroom requirements ahead of time will make the experience more comfortable for everyone.

Students With a Disability Ought to Know:

67. that **distance learning courses may provide a good option for students with attendance and participation issues.** Remember that distance learning courses require self-discipline to keep up and be successful. Please be certain to check the formats used for the course if you are using assistive technology such as screen readers to make sure it is going to work for you. You may want to review the book *100 Things Every Online Student Ought to Know.* For more information, see www.cambridgestratford.com/online_learning/index.html .

Students With a Disability Ought to Know:

68.   that a **request for extension of time to complete assignments or programs might be a reasonable accommodation in some circumstances.** Make your need known to your instructor as soon as possible. Instructors are less likely to approve such a request if you wait until the last minute to ask for an extension. The DSS office can help by advocating on your behalf. Often more time will not be granted to finish assignments that are announced very early in the class or are listed on the syllabus.

Students With a Disability Ought to Know:

69. that **maintaining an open line of communication with your instructors is good practice** for any student, and is particularly important for students with disabilities. Instructors can't help if you don't let them know what is going on. You shouldn't hesitate to educate faculty and staff about your disability. Professors want to know how best to assist you, and may often ask how they can help to meet your needs. Remember that you should avoid labeling yourself as an underachiever when talking with your college professors. Focus on your strengths, not your weaknesses.

"You don't need a MEMO to talk on your behalf. Professors are cool if you just take the time to talk to them." Mark, senior, blind

Students With a Disability Ought to Know:

70. that **lab assistants or classroom assistants may be provided for students with mobility or visual impairments,** especially in science-related courses. A pre-assessment may be needed, so talk with the instructor and the DSS office as soon as possible.

LABORATORY RETRIEVER

Students With a Disability Ought to Know:

71.   that you should **ensure a good experience for your service animal and your classmates.** Service animals are welcome on campus. Assess the classroom environment to ensure convenience and safety, especially for maintaining a clear path of travel for others, and a safe place for your animal. If you use assistive devices or other technology in the classroom, please be respectful of others and don't disrupt the learning environment for others in the class. For example, talking watches and other devices can be distracting in some learning environments.

Students With a Disability Ought to Know:

72.   that if you are having difficulty in a particular course, you may want to **consider pass/fail and no credit options** if available at your institution. In some circumstances, a course substitution may be considered an appropriate accommodation and may be preferred over a course waiver. Being granted a course substitution may require petitions and a lengthy process. Course substitutions are generally considered only in exceptional circumstances. Check with the DSS office regarding your institution's policy.

Students With a Disability Ought to Know:

73.   that **auditing a course is a great way to brainstorm about how to accommodate your particular needs** before you take the course for a grade. There may be a charge for officially auditing a course. Successful classroom experiences can depend on creativity and cooperation. Sometimes observing actual classroom requirements can provide the most insight for you.

"Don't let anyone tell you that you can't do it—It took me 7 years but I did it." Mary, graduate, cerebral palsy, wheelchair user

Chapter 4 Worksheet

Critical components for academic success are listed below. Check each item that you have completed.

_____ I have reviewed the academic requirements and technical standards for my chosen program of study.

_____ I have affirmed my ability to meet those requirements and standards with reasonable accommodations.

_____ I have discussed my field of study and accommodations with an academic advisor for my program.

_____ I have discussed my accommodation needs relative to my course of study with the DSS office.

_____ I have delivered the advocacy memo from the DSS Office and discussed my accommodations for each course with the instructor.

_____ I have reviewed the syllabus for each course.

_____ If testing accommodations have been approved, I have discussed these accommodations with my instructors.

_____ I have visited the classroom to ensure it is accessible for my needs.

_____ I have requested special physical arrangements in the classroom (i.e. adjustable table, room for service animal, preferred seating, etc.) These are

_____

_____

_____

_____ I need a classroom assistant, lab assistant or sign language interpreter.

_____ I have arranged for this service.   Date _____

_____ I will need alternative format text/course materials.

_____ I have arranged for/ordered these materials. Date _____

Date needed _____ Anticipated date of delivery _____

_____ I have a plan for accessing/producing materials for homework.

5 | Campus Life

Students With a Disability Ought to Know:

74. that **college life includes more than academics**. Involvement in campus extra-curricular activities can round out your academic experience and provide a welcome break from the stresses of academic life. Remember, all campus activities are to be made accessible to students with disabilities.

"I never knew how much fun being involved in student organizations could be because I didn't get involved in high school. If time allows, join a student organization. I became president of LSA and it has helped networking for work." Jessie, Senior, learning disability

Students With a Disability Ought to Know:

75. that **the experience gained from joining a student organization is priceless.** Don't feel as if you must limit yourself to joining the disabled student organization on your campus. Seek out organizations that match your particular interests and passions. Of course, participation in the disabled student organization is an excellent way to bring about change on your campus. If your campus does not have such an organization and you have leadership skills, consider establishing one. National organizations such as the National Disabled Students

Union (www2.uic.edu/stud_orgs/pol/dsu/) or the Canadian-based National Educational Association of Disabled Students (www.neads.ca/) can provide guidance in establishing an organization at your institution.

"Consider all your needs in college, not just your disability-related ones." Sarah, senior, visually impaired

Students With a Disability Ought to Know:

76. that **navigating the campus climate and attitudes can be intimidating for some students with severe and visible disabilities**. Will I be accepted? Will professors treat me differently? Will my peers and roommates relate to me? Will I fail? Will I make friends? Will my roommate and I have things in common? Remember that these are typical concerns expressed by all students, not just by students with disabilities. Overcoming fear and self-doubt and getting involved in campus life will be the first step to feeling included.

Students With a Disability Ought to Know:

77. that **finding a good roommate match is a challenge for all students, but can be significantly more challenging for students with disabilities**. Students should be comfortable with explaining their disabilities to others to avoid misconceptions and stereotypes.

"My roommate seemed uncomfortable that I was in a wheelchair when we first met. Ultimately, we became best of friends and he was thankful that we had one of the biggest rooms on the floor." Steven, freshman, wheelchair user

Students With a Disability Ought to Know:

78. that **you should not expect your college roommate to provide special services for you.** Roommates should not be used as your therapist, your personal care attendant, or mobility assistant. Your DSS office may be able to provide you with assistance in arranging for these personal needs with outside sources. Students who use wheelchairs, white canes, or have other mobility concerns may have difficulty navigating cafeteria lines. Food service staff are generally very willing to assist students in the cafeterias. Talk with the DSS office or your residence hall director about your particular needs and expectations.

Students With a Disability Ought to Know:

79. that **students with service animals, significant medical needs, or extenuating circumstances may qualify for a single residence hall room.** Requests are reviewed on an individual basis. Students who use personal care assistants, or who have concerns about community bathrooms and privacy issues, should talk with their residence life director or DSS office regarding on-campus housing options.

"Live on campus. It's a great part of the whole experience." Heather, *sophomore, wheelchair user*

Students With a Disability Ought to Know:

80. that **a service animal is any animal individually trained to do work or perform tasks for the benefit of a person with a disability.** A service animal may alert a person with impaired hearing to the presence of people or sounds. The animal may assist a person with mobility impairments by pulling a wheelchair, retrieving dropped items, turning on lights, or otherwise helping with specific tasks. Service animals are usually dogs, but may include other animals with appropriate training.

Students With a Disability Ought to Know:

81. that **pets are not service animals.** As much as many students would like to have their pets stay with them, colleges generally have strict guidelines for allowing animals in residence halls or on campus. A person with a disability uses a service animal as an auxiliary aid similar to the use of a cane, crutches, or a wheelchair.

Students With a Disability Ought to Know:

82. that you should **learn evacuation procedures existing on your campus** for students with disabilities. In the aftermath of 9-11, many schools have adopted evacuation procedures that specifically address the needs of students with disabilities. In the event that your school does not have a formal evacuation procedure, make your own plan. Consult with the DSS office about how to design a plan for yourself. Deaf and hard of hearing students should check the availability of visual alarms, and, if living in a residence hall, coordinate a plan with the residence life director.

Students With a Disability Ought to Know:

83. that **behavior and performance count**. All students—with or without disabilities—are expected to follow the student code of conduct. Disability is no excuse for breaking the rules or not respecting the rights of others.

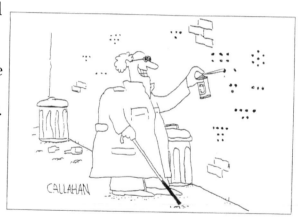

Students With a Disability Ought to Know:

84. that **many college campuses offer intramural sports programs that are or can be fully adaptable for participation by students with disabilities.** Organizations such as Wheelchair Sports, USA (www.wsusa.org) and the NSW Wheelchair Sports Association (www.nswwsa.org.au) may be able to provide guidance in developing programs at your campus if none are offered.

Students With a Disability Ought to Know:

85. that **participation in study abroad programs can make you much more marketable when looking for employment after graduation**. Students with disabilities should disclose their disability needs to program staff early and remember that other cultures will vary in the way they provide and support disability access. You will likely encounter a different way of dealing with your disability abroad and a different degree of independence than you are accustomed to. Thus, students considering study abroad programs should be flexible and be prepared to do extensive advance planning. The DSS

office and your college campus abroad office can assist you in determining the type of accommodations that may be possible at your selected site. For additional information and resources on study abroad planning for students with disabilities, visit Mobility International USA at www.miusa.org/.

"The best advice I can give, particularly to those whose disabilities are more severe than mine, is to plan well in advance. Access was much different in the country I studied but the experience of studying abroad was worth it." Angela, senior, mobility impaired

Chapter 5 Worksheet

A great college experience involves more than academics. Take a moment to identify those areas that are important to you and your particular needs. Check all that apply.

_____ The college has student organizations that meet my interests.
Organizations I'm considering joining or exploring include:

_____

_____

_____

_____ The college offers intramural sports that are accessible to my needs.

_____ The college offers study abroad opportunities.

Residential students:

_____ The college is able to accommodate my special housing needs. These needs
include:_____

_____

_____

_____

_____ I have met with the residence hall director to discuss any special needs or
concerns.

_____ I am aware of the college emergency evacuation plans for students with
disabilities.

_____ I have identified an area to exercise my service animal.

6 Success Strategies

Students With a Disability Ought to Know:

86.   that **good study skills are very important and can be the key to your academic success**. You should know how to study on your own. If you don't know how to study, or if the way you are studying is not effective, there are many sources of help. Sign up for a study skills course, attend workshops, and find resources on the web. Go to http://studygs.net or www.cambridgestratford.com .

Students With a Disability Ought to Know:

87.   that **some colleges offer summer transition programs for college-bound freshmen with disabilities.** These programs are designed to give students a "head start" or a first-hand look at the postsecondary college experience in preparation for the transition to higher learning. Some of these programs provide students the opportunity to participate in college courses, receive study skills training, self-advocacy skill building, and test-taking strategies. Programs can vary from a few days to a full week. The HEATH Resource Center, a national clearinghouse on postsecondary education for individuals with disabilities, maintains a listing of available programs.

You can visit them at http://www.heath.gwu.edu
Also, many colleges offer a freshman-year experience course
or college survival course that can help you learn the campus
resources available, in addition to study skills and test-taking
skills. Take advantage of these opportunities to find out
important information early on.

Students With a Disability Ought to Know:

88. that you need to plan on **at least three hours or more for homework per class hour** if you have a disability that will require you to spend more time completing assignments. Keep in mind that all students should plan on spending two to three hours doing assignments outside of class for every hour spent in the classroom, so you may need to allow for extra time. This is very important when planning your class schedule, as well as trying to fit in a job and/or family obligations.

Students With a Disability Ought to Know:

89.   that **you should find a good place on campus to study**. Dorms can be noisy and distracting. If you are a commuter student, try to schedule time on campus to study. There can be too many conflicting obligations once you get home to allow you the time and space you need to concentrate.

Students With a Disability Ought to Know:

90. that **if you don't use technology—especially computers—learn as quickly as you can**. Using computers will be required to get through nearly any college program, and technology may be one of the keys to your success. It is difficult to learn how to use a computer, learn specialized software or equipment, and learn course material all at the same time.

"If you are blind like me, learn the computer before you come to college. It will make things easier." Maidi, senior, communication major, international student

Students With a Disability Ought to Know:

91.   that **knowing your learning style is important**, especially when you are selecting classes and instructors, and using study techniques. Do you learn better when you hear information rather than read it? Do you learn better when you can do things "hands on?" In other words, what works best for you? Understand your learning strengths and apply those styles of learning to your study routine. For a quick on-line learning style assessment visit,
http://www.ldpride.net/learningstyles.MI.htm .

Students With a Disability Ought to Know:

92.   that **participating in group study sessions is an excellent way to establish a relationship with classmates**. It also is a way to learn study techniques that are effective for other students. Mixing group study time with individual study can be very helpful to those who find it difficult to concentrate or stay on task for long periods of time.

Students With a Disability Ought to Know:

93.   that **good communication and self-advocacy skills are essential**. You will be the primary shaper of your academic experience.   Don't be afraid to insist on your rights. Be assertive in stating your needs; however, be willing to collaborate and try suggestions. Aggressiveness can be viewed as confrontational and threatening. Work to keep positive communication with faculty, staff and your peers.

Students With a Disability Ought to Know:

94.   that **being organized can make a huge difference**, especially for students with ADD, brain injuries, or certain psychological conditions.   Color-coding folders for all notes and course materials by subject, establishing specific places to put supplies, assignments, and completed work, and carefully setting out each night what is needed for the next day can help get you out the door tomorrow morning.

Students With a Disability Ought to Know:

95.   that **planners and/or PDAs (hand-held organiz-ers)** should be used by all students, but especially by students with memory deficits or who have difficulty focusing. You need to plan your time, including setting aside enough time for study as well as recreation. These tools can make the difference for meeting your obligations and being successful. Discipline and time management must be a priority.

Students With a Disability Ought to Know:

96.   that **you shouldn't be too proud to ask for assistance.** Asking for assistance is encouraged and expected. Student services, such as the DSS office, career counseling, and tutoring departments exist for this very reason—to provide support to help you succeed.

"I didn't want to use accommodations or ask for help because I didn't want to be 'different.' It was a matter of pride. Then I saw my poor mid-term grades. I'm much smarter now; I use the resources that are here." Becky, business major, learning disability

Students With a Disability Ought to Know:

97.   that **dropping a course does not indicate a failure**. Some students may experience unpredictable difficulties, such as students with chronic health conditions or mental illness. Therefore, you may need to adjust your course load as you go. Dropping a course signifies a realistic self-assessment of what you can accomplish at that time. This holds equally true if you find you have to leave school temporarily because of medical conditions. Most schools have a medical leave policy that can assist you with your withdrawal. Also, the drop and add period may be an excellent opportunity to check out different instructors to see if their teaching style matches with your learning strengths. Become familiar with the drop and add deadlines at your institution.

Students With a Disability Ought to Know:

98.   that if you have **problems with a foreign language because of a documented language-based learning disability**, you may be allowed to substitute courses that provide knowledge of other cultures. Institutional policies about foreign language substitutions vary, so check with the DSS office about this option.

Students With a Disability Ought to Know:

99. that **finding a mentor can ease your college experience**. A good mentor can be a more experienced student with a disability, a faculty member, a staff person, or a member of the community. This person may offer advice, provide guidance for navigating the system, help you find resources, or make connections in the community. A mentor can often become a life-long friend, and is an important part of your support system.

Students With a Disability Ought to Know:

100. that **you need to become familiar with the library and the resources available**. If you need an alternative means to access the catalog listings, references, text, or electronic or archived information, speak with the librarians about your needs. The DSS office can assist in finding solutions to your access needs. You will most certainly need to do research for many of your courses, and being familiar with using the library will give you a head start.

Students With a Disability Ought to Know:

101. that **you should learn to manage stress, recognize depression, and resolve conflicts**. Learning to keep these factors under control will help you focus on academics. If any of these become a problem, get help from the counseling office or another treatment provider as soon as possible. Being aware of strategies to recognize and cope with stress, depression and conflict will be valuable in your other campus and family relationships as well as for your own well-being. At some institutions, stress-management workshops may be provided by the counseling office.

Students With a Disability Ought to Know:

102. that **you need to work toward independence and self-reliance in as many areas as possible.** There won't be a DSS office once you leave the college setting, so don't over-accommodate or rely heavily on services from others. Develop your own self-accommodation strategies, and learn to access your own materials. Technology is a great benefit to many people with disabilities because of the level of independence it offers.

Chapter 6 Worksheet

There are a number of success strategies that students can use to meet their needs.
Check the ones you feel are most important for your academic success.

___ Assistance with learning good study skills.

  The college offers a study skills class.   Yes ❏   No ❏

___ Assistance with mastering effective note-taking techniques.

  The college offers workshops or tutorials on
  effective note-taking.   Yes ❏   No ❏

___ Assistance with effective test-taking strategies.

  The college offers workshops or tutorials
  on effective test-taking.   Yes ❏   No ❏

___ Assistance with time-management and organizational skills.

> The college offers workshops or tutorials on
> time-management.   Yes ❏   No ❏

> I use a planner or PDA to schedule my time.   Yes ❏   No ❏

___ Tutoring assistance for subject areas.

> The college provides free subject area tutoring.   Yes ❏   No ❏

> Tutors are trained in working with students
> with various disabilities   Yes ❏   No ❏

___ Assistance with increasing math skills.

   The college offers developmental courses in math.   Yes ❑   No ❑

___ Assistance with improving reading skills.

   The college offers developmental courses in reading.   Yes ❑   No ❑

___ Assistance with improving writing skills.

   The college offers developmental courses in writing.   Yes ❑   No ❑

7 Transitions: Moving On

Students With a Disability Ought to Know:

103. that **not all colleges will be able to meet your needs.** Some colleges may have a greater population of individuals with your particular disability, and may have more expertise providing the type and level of assistance you need. In fact, students transfer to other institutions for many reasons. Don't hesitate to explore your options if your current situation is not working for you.

Students With a Disability Ought to Know:

104. that when **considering transferring to another college or attending graduate school**, the same process for becoming eligible for accommodations will apply. Update your disability documentation if it is no longer current. Do your homework and make sure the institution is what you are looking for *before* you enroll. Visit the campus, and talk with the DSS staff and currently enrolled students with disabilities.

Students With a Disability Ought to Know:

105. that **students with disabilities are entitled to the same legal protection in graduate and professional schools**. However, some will place much more scrutiny on the definition of disability when determining eligibility for accommodations. Remember, to receive an accommodation, your disability must be "substantially limiting" when compared to the average person.

Students With a Disability Ought to Know:

106. that if you are pursuing graduate or professional studies, **your disability may make you eligible for accommodations on national entrance exams**, such as the GRE, GMAT, LSAT and others. Check out the Educational Testing Services website at www.ets.org to determine eligibility and documentation requirements. In many instances, the disability documentation requirements may be more stringent than for undergraduate programs. Students should work with the DSS office early on to establish a history of using accommodations for college tests.

Students With a Disability Ought to Know:

107. that **you shouldn't wait until you are near graduation to make use of the campus Career Services office.** Many colleges have developed excellent services to assist students with disabilities in their career and vocational needs. Getting answers to questions such as how and when to disclose your disability in an interview, when to ask an employer for accommodations, or who pays for workplace accommodations, are issues that Career Services should be able to address. On some campuses, the Career Services and DSS offices provide workshops for students that specifically address these concerns.

Students With a Disability Ought to Know:

108. that when **preparing for employment after graduation, focus on your ability with potential employers, not your disability**. Be prepared to tell a potential employer how you can do the job and how you can accomplish the essential functions of the job as stated in the job description. If you will need adaptive equipment or special technology, be informed about the approximate cost and where it is made available.

Students With a Disability Ought to Know:

109. that **campus work, co-ops, and internships are a must** for all students in today's competitive world, but even more so for students with disabilities. Demonstrating your work ability before graduation goes a long way to dispel myths and stereotypes that exist in the workplace about individuals with disabilities.

Students With a Disability Ought to Know:

110. that you **can use your involvement in campus organizations to connect to similar groups in the community.** For example, if you belonged to a campus group involved in service activities, you can make a connection with many of the widely known service organizations in most every community (Kiwanis, Optimists, Lions, Rotary, etc.).

Students With a Disability Ought to Know:

111. that in the grand scheme of things, **it's about ability, not disability**. Like every journey in life, college and the transition to life beyond college is about choice, not chance. Choose to find guidance along the way. Use the information in this book as one of many tools to help you reach your goals.

Chapter 7 Worksheet

If you are considering transferring to another institution, entering graduate school, or moving on to a job, check the items that pertain to your choice and complete the necessary information.

_____ I am considering transferring to another college.

Schools I am considering are: _____

_____

_____

_____ I have researched the above schools and the programs/services offered will meet my needs.

_____ I have current (within three years) documentation of my disability.

_____ I will need to take entrance exams. They are:_____

_____

_____ I will need accommodations for these exams. These are: _____

_____

_____ I have submitted the required paperwork requesting accommodations.

Date submitted:_____   Confirmation received:_____

Date of test:_____   Location: _____

_____ I have explored career options with the Career Services office.

_____ I have participated in campus employment, co-op placements, and/or internships.

Position: _____ Contact:_____

Office/Agency/Business Name: _____

Position: _____ Contact:_____

Office/Agency/Business Name: _____

_____ I will need adaptive equipment or special technology on the job. These are:

_____Source_____Cost _____

_____Source_____Cost _____

_____Source_____Cost _____

Appendix

Editor Contribution Form

Dear Reader,

Your comments can help other students with a disablitiy make a smoother transition to college. Please share your thoughts, ideas, and suggestions on the following pages or on a separate sheet of paper. Also, fill in the biographical information below. We'll include a special reference by-line in our next edition to acknowledge all contributors. Thank you!

Name _____

Institution _____

City _____ State _____ Zip _____

- [ ] *Student*
- [ ] *Faculty*
- [ ] *Administrator*
- [ ] *Family/Friend*
- [ ] _____

(Cut or tear out form or e-mail to Cambridges@aol.com)

My thoughts, ideas, and suggestions are

_____

_____

_____

_____

_____

_____

_____

_____

_____

_____

_____

_____

(Cut or tear out form or e-mail to Cambridges@aol.com)

_____

_____

_____

_____

_____

_____

_____

_____

_____

Mail To: Kendra Johnson and Trudie Hines
              c/o The Cambridge Stratford Study Skills Institute
              8560 Main Street
              Williamsville, NY 14221

(Cut or tear out form or e-mail to Cambridges@aol.com)

Glossary of Terms

504 Plan: a written plan falling under the provisions of the Rehabilitation Act of 1973. It is designed to provide instructional and environmental accommodations for students with health conditions or disabilities not covered under IDEA in public K-12 schools. A 504 Plan is for students in regular education, and is not an Individualized Education Program (IEP) as is required for special education students.

Accommodations: a modification to academic requirements as necessary to ensure that such requirements do not discriminate against students with disabilities, or have the effect of excluding students solely on the basis of disability. Modifications are extended to policies, practices, procedures and activities relating to all campus programs and activities.

Advocacy Memo: a written correspondence from the DSS office to a faculty member verifying student need for classroom accommodations. The memo will generally state what accommodations may be reasonable, how they will be provided, as well as each party's role (student, professor, and DSS office) in the accommodation process.

Americans with Disabilities Act (ADA): prohibits discrimination against persons with disabilities in employment, public services, and places of public accommodations. It is the most comprehensive federal civil-rights statute protecting the rights of persons with disabilities. The U.S. Department of Education Office for Civil Rights (OCR) and the Equal Employment Opportunity Commission (EEOC) are the governing bodies responsible for compliance with the ADA for colleges and universities.

Assistive Devices and Technology: equipment that promotes capability in handling a wider range of activities with greater independence for students with disabilities. Examples would be large print displays on computer screens for students with a visual impairment; computer voice output for students with a reading disability; and alternative keyboards and pointing devices for students with mobility impairments. For more information, see http://www.abledata.com or www.ataccess.org .

Audit: registering in a credit class and attending regularly but generally not taking examinations. Auditing a class means that the class will not count for credit or grade point average. In some cases, the audit fee is less than the tuition rate. Registration for audit may require the permission of the instructor.

C-Print: a speech-to-text system developed at the National Technical Institute for the Deaf (NTID), a college of Rochester Institute of Technology (RIT), as a communication access service option for some deaf and hard-of-hearing students in educational environments. A trained operator produces text of the spoken information using text-condensing strategies and an abbreviation system. The text can be displayed simultaneously to one or more students using additional computers (laptops) or display monitors. The captionist generally provides a meaning-for-meaning (not verbatim) translation of the spoken English content. This system also can be used for students with other disabilities. For more information see http://cprint.rit.edu . There are also other similar products available.

Center for Independent Living (CIL): service organizations designed specifically to assist people with disabilities in achieving and maintaining independent lifestyles. Centers for independent living are run by people with disabilities who themselves have been successful in establishing independent lives. The first center was formed in 1972 in Berkeley, California. Title VII of the Rehabilitation Act provided federal funding to establish independent living centers and today there are centers in virtually every state and U.S. territory. For a directory of centers, see http:// www.bcm.tmc.edu/ilru/jump1.htm .

Disability: any person who, as defined by the ADA, (1) has a physical or mental impairment which <u>substantially limits</u> one or more <u>major life activities</u>, (2) has a history of having such an impairment, or (3) is regarded as having an impairment. Major life activities include walking, seeing, hearing, speaking, breathing, learning, working, caring for oneself, and performing manual tasks.

Disability Support Services (DSS): college support and advocacy services for students with disabilities. This service may go by various names depending on the individual college (such as Disabled Student Services, Access Services, Office of Accessibility). To receive these services, a person with a disability must make a request to the DSS office and provide documentation regarding the disability.

Documentation of Disability: relative to a student with a disability requesting services at a college, this is a written assessment from a professional with expertise in that particular field of disability. This documentation of the disability is required to determine the student's eligibility for accommodations and the specific accommodations needed based on the student's current limitations.

Drop and Add Period: the time frame when students can make changes to their class schedule. Generally courses may be changed prior to the beginning of a semester or session and, sometimes, during the first few days of the term.

Electronic Text: is text stored in a file format which may be opened and used on a computer or other similar technology, especially for access by screen readers or needed for conversion to other formats such as Braille.

Equal Access: provides students with disabilities who are "otherwise qualified" the same educational opportunities and full participation in programs and activities provided to all other students.

Family Educational Rights to Privacy Act (FERPA): a federal law that affords students certain rights concerning their student record. The law is known as FERPA or the Buckley Amendment. For more information, see www.ed.gov/offices/OM/fpco/ferpa .

Individuals with Disabilities Education Act (IDEA): a special education law designed to provide federal assistance to state and local K-12 agencies to guarantee special education and related services to eligible children with disabilities. Under

IDEA, eligible students are entitled to a free and appropriate education in the least restrictive environment. For more information, see www.ed.gov/about/offices/list/osers/osep/index.html or http://www.fape.org/index.htm .

Individualized Education Program (IEP): specially designed instruction and related services identified in a written plan for students receiving special education services in K-12 as required by IDEA. For more information see http://www.fape.org/index.htm or http://www.ed.gov/parents/needs/speced/iepguide/index.html .

MP3 Files: a file encoding format for audio files. Often used for music, these files can also support voice files. Some screen-reading programs can save computer voice files in this format so that text can be converted and played on any device supporting the format.

No Credit Option: see "Audit"

Orientation: a program designed for incoming freshmen providing a formal introduction to the campus, its policies, and procedures. Students will typically meet with their assigned academic advisors and register for their fall semester classes. Separate orientation programs may be offered for adult or transfer students.

Orientation and Mobility Training: teaches orientation skills used to find one's way in an environment and mobility skills used to travel independently primarily for persons with vision impairments. Such training is usually provided by a trained Orientation and Mobility (O & M) Specialist.

Otherwise Qualified: see "Qualified Person with a Disability"

Pass – Fail Option: a student attends the class regularly and completes all work and examinations. If a "pass" grade is received, the class counts for credit but no grade is computed in the grade point average. Options and restrictions will vary, so check with your program advisors.

Personal Services: assistance of a personal nature for individuals with disabilities that are not required to be provided under the ADA. These may include such things as personal care attendants, personal tutors, transportation, speech therapy, occupational therapy, and personal devices.

Priority Registration: an accommodation that allows a student with a disability-related need the opportunity to register for a class early to ensure availability. Typical circumstances include having a medical condition that limits the time of day in which a student can effectively participate, dependence on special transportation that has limited scheduling flexibility, or the need to plan for alternative format class materials well in advance.

Qualified Person with Disability: a person with a disability who, as defined by federal disability law, meets the academic and technical standards required for admission or participation in an education program or activity, with or without accommodations.

Reasonable Accommodations: any accommodation which provides equal access to a student with a disability. Accommodations are considered to be reasonable if they do not cross the line for "unreasonable" as defined by the ADA.

Section 504 of the 1973 Rehabilitation Act: a civil rights law designed to prohibit discrimination on the basis of disability in programs and activities that receive federal financial assistance. The law specifically states:

> *No <u>otherwise qualified persons with a disability</u> in the United States...shall, solely by reason of disability, be denied the benefits of, be excluded from participation in, or be subjected to discrimination under any program or activity receiving financial assistance....*

Note: The Americans with Disabilities Act (ADA) of 1990 extends the provisions of Section 504 to private colleges, regardless of whether they receive federal funding. Most colleges and universities in the United State are subject to one or both of these laws.

Self-Advocacy: the ability to speak up for yourself, ask for the things you need and want, stand up for your rights, and take responsibility for your actions. To become an effective self-advocate, a student with a disability must understand his/her particular disability, how it impacts learning, and become comfortable with describing to others the disability and related academic needs.

Services: see "Personal Services"

Service Animals: any animal individually or professionally trained to do work or perform tasks for the benefit of a person with a disability. A service animal may alert a person with impaired hearing to the presence of people or sounds. An animal may assist a person with mobility impairments by pulling a wheelchair, retrieving dropped items, turning on lights, or otherwise helping with specific tasks. Service animals are usually dogs, but may include other animals with appropriate training

Scan and Read Programs: computer programs that allow users to scan text with a scanner and have it converted to voice output by using optical character recognition (OCR) technology.

Screen Readers: software that will "read" text files. Voice output is computer-generated.

Syllabus: a written summary of the expectations of a college course which will include the course description, learning objectives, reading assignments and due dates, quiz and test dates, grading criteria, and faculty contact information.

Substitution: a replacement of a class required for completion of a degree or program with another class. The substitution may be granted to a student with a disability if the student's disability documentation supports the need for a class substitution and the substitution does not alter an essential or necessary element of the academic program.

Technical Standards: standards for successful participation in a program or course of study which may include subjective evaluative measures or physical requirements.

Transcript: a copy of a student's permanent record, including courses attempted and grades.

Vocational Rehabilitation (VR): state agencies that receive federal funding to provide employment-related services to individuals with disabilities, giving priority to individuals with significant disabilities. www.jan.wvu.edu/SBSES/VOCREHAB.htm

Voice Recognition: technology that allows users to dictate and have their spoken words appear on a screen or monitor.

Waiver: an agreement that a specific class which is a component of a degree or certificate program is not required for a particular student. A waiver is rarely granted and should not be expected. A waiver may be granted to a student with a disability if the student's disability documentation supports the need for a waiver, a reasonable accommodation for completing the course cannot be identified, an appropriate course substitution cannot be found, and the waiver would not alter an essential or necessary part of the program.

Works Consulted

Brinckerhoff, L., McGuire, J., & Shaw, S. (2001). *Postsecondary education and transition for students with learning disabilities.* PRO-ED, Inc.

Brinckerhoff, L., Shaw, S., & McGuire, J. (1992). Promoting access, accommodations, and independence for college students with learning disabilities. *Journal of Learning Disabilities,* 25, 417-429.

Burgstahler, S. (2003). The role of technology in preparing youth with disabilities for postsecondary education and employment. *Journal of Special Education Technology,* 18 (4), 7-19.

Bursuck, W. & Rose, E. (1992). Community college options for students with mild disabilities. In F.R. Rusch, et al. (Eds.). *Transition from school to life.* Sycamore, Illinois: Sycamore Publishing.

Johnson, D. (2000). Enhancing out-of-class opportunities for students with disabilities. In H.A. Belch (Ed.). *Serving students with disabilities.* New Directions for Student Services, no. 91. San Francisco, California: Jossey-Bass.

Lynch, R. & Gussel, L. (1996). Disclosure and self-advocacy regarding disability-related need: Strategies to maximize integration in post-secondary education. *Journal of Counseling and Development*, 74, 352-357.

Pierangelo, R. & Crane, R. (1997). *Complete guide to special education transition services.* West Nyack, New York: The Center for Applied Research in Education.

Simon, J. (2000). Legal issues in serving students with disabilities in postsecondary Education. In H.A. Belch (ed.). *Serving students with disabilities.* New Directions for Student Services, no. 91. San Francisco, California: Jossey-Bass.

Wolanin, T. R. & Steele, P. E. (2004). *Higher education opportunities for students with disabilities: A primer for policymakers*. Washington D.C.: The Institute for Higher Education Policy.

Suggested Student Readings

Brinckerhoff, L. (2002). *College students with learning disabilities.* [Brochure]. Massachusetts: Association on Higher Education and Disability.

Disbro, W. (1995). *100 things every college freshmen ought to know.* Williamsville, New York: The Cambridge Stratford Study Skills Institute.

Mooney, J. & Cole, D. (2000). *Learning outside the lines: Two ivy league students with learning disabilities and ADHD give you the tools for academic success and educational revolution.* New York: Fireside.

Quinn, P. (Ed.). (2001). *ADD and the college student: A guide for high school and college students with attention deficit disorder.* Washington D.C.: Magination Press

Peterson's. (2003). *Colleges with programs for students with learning disabilities or attention deficit disorders, 7th edition.* New Jersey: Thomson Peterson's .

The Association on Higher Education and Disability. (2003). *College students who are deaf or hard of hearing.* [Brochure]. Massachusetts: Association on Higher Education and Disability.

The Association on Higher Education and Disability. (2002). *College students who have ADHD.* [Brochure]. Massachusetts: Association on Higher Education and Disability.

The Association on Higher Education and Disability. (2002). *College students who have chronic diseases or medical conditions.* [Brochure]. Massachusetts: Association on Higher Education and Disability.

The Association on Higher Education and Disability. (2001). *Confidentiality & disability issues in higher education.* [Brochure]. Massachusetts: Association on Higher Education and Disability.

The Association on Higher Education and Disability. (2003). *Preparing for college: Options for students with learning disabilities.* [Brochure]. Massachusetts: Association on Higher Education and Disability.

The Association on Higher Education and Disability. (2002). *Ready, set, go: Helping students with learning disabilities prepare for college.* [Brochure]. Massachusetts: Association on Higher Education and Disability.

The Association on Higher Education and Disability. (2002). *Section 504: The law and its impact on postsecondary education.* [Brochure]. Massachusetts: Association on Higher Education and Disability.

The Association on Higher Education and Disability. (2002). *The Americans with Disabilities Act: The law and its impact on postsecondary education.* [Brochure]. Massachusetts: Association on Higher Education and Disability.

U.S. Department of Education. (2002). *Students with disabilities preparing for postsecondary education: Know your rights and responsibilities.* Washington, D.C.

Webliography

ABLEDATA – http://www.abledata.com
Resource for assistive technology

Academic Success, Inc. - http://www.academicsuccess.com
Publisher of books and aids on math study skills

ACT - http://www.act.org/
The ACT college entrance exam, assessments, educational and career planning

Association on Higher Education and Disability(AHEAD) - http://ahead.org/
An international organization promoting excellence through education, communication and training. Founded in 1977, AHEAD addresses the need and concern for upgrading the quality of services and support available to persons with disabilities in higher education.

Alliance for Technology Access – www.ataccess.org
> A network of community-based resource centers, developers and vendors dedicated to providing information and support services to children and adults with disabilities, and increasing their use of standard, assistive and information technologies.

Americans with Disabilities Act (ADA) - http://www.usdoj.gov/crt/ada.
> U. S. Department of Justice website providing ADA information.

Cambridge Stratford Study Skills Institute - http://www.cambridgestratford.com
> Publisher of study skills and college orientation guides.

Centers for Independent Living - http://www.bcm.tmc.edu/ilru/jump1.htm
> Listing of centers throughout the Unites States

Educational Testing Service organization (ETS) - http://ets.org/
> Organization that provides the SAT college entrance exam.

Family and Advocates Partnership for Education - http://www.fape.org

> Provides information to educate families and advocates about the Individuals with Disabilities Education Act (IDEA). Also includes information about transition from secondary to post-secondary settings.

Family Educational Rights to Privacy Act (FERPA) -
> http://www.ed.gov/offices/OM/fpco/ferpa
> U.S. Department of Education website for FERPA information.

HEATH Resource Center—National Clearinghouse on Postsecondary Education for Individuals with Disabilities - http://www.heath.gwu.edu/

> Heath serves as an information exchange about educational support services, policies, procedures, adaptations, and opportunities at American campuses, vocational/technical schools, and other postsecondary training entities.

IDEA, ADA and Section 504 - http://education.state.mn.us/mde/static/000196.pfd
Comparison of IDEA, ADA and Section 504 pertaining to education

IDEA, ADA and Section 504 - http://www.cgc.maricopa.edu/disability/pdf/acts.pdf
Chart comparing these laws as they pertain to education

Kurzweil Educational Systems - http://www.kurzweiledu.com
Kurzweil scan/read software

LD Pride – www.ldpride.net/learningstyles.MI.htm
On-line learning style assessment

Mobility International USA - http://www.miusa.org/
A national clearinghouse that educates people with disabilities and related organizations about the international exchange opportunities.

National Center for Educational Statistics - http://nces.ed.gov/
A primary federal entity for collecting and analyzing data related to education in the United States.

National Disabled Students Union - http://www2.uic.edu/stud_orgs/pol/dsu
An Australian-based organization offering opportunities for people with disabilities to enjoy the benefits of recreation.

National Educational Association of Disabled Students - http://www.neads.ca/
Canadian-based organization for students with disabilities.

NSW Wheelchair Sports Association - http://www.nswwsa.org.au

Office for Civil Rights (OCR) - http://www.ed.gov/ocr/docs/howto.html
The U.S. Department of Education website which includes information on how to file a discrimination complaint

Peterson's Guide to Colleges - http://www.petersons.com/
   Publisher of educational resources and guides pertaining to college.

Read Please - http://www.readplease.com/
   Scan/read software

Recording for the Blind and Dyslexic (RFB & D) – http://www.rfbd.org/
   A national nonprofit organization serving people who cannot read standard print because of a disability. RFB&D is a library of academic and professional textbooks on audio tape or electronic text from elementary through post-graduate and professional levels.

Study Guides and Strategies - http://studygs.net
   Study skills online source

Summer Pre-college Programs -
   http://www.heath.gwu.edu
   Listing of summer pre-college programs for students with disabilities

Vocational Rehabilitation Offices -
http://www.jan.wvu.edu/SBSES/VOCREHAB.htm
State-by-state listing.

Wheelchair Sports, USA - http://www.wsusa.org
A organization led by wheelchair athletes that is dedicated to the guidance and development of wheelchair sports.

Additional Web Resources for Assisting College Students with Disabilities *

ADA Watch - http://www.adawatch.org
The ADA Watch is a non-profit informational online network to inform the disability community of threats to civil rights protections for people with disabilities.

Adaptive Environments, Inc. - http://www.adaptenv.org/

> A non-profit organization founded in 1978 to address the environmental issues that confront people with disabilities and elderly people. Adaptive Environments promotes accessibility as well as universal design through education programs, technical assistance, training, consulting, publications and design advocacy.

American Printing House for the Blind - http://www.aph.org/

> Provides materials, alternative media, tools, and resources for individuals who are blind or visually impaired.

Americans with Disabilities Act Document Center -
http://www.jan.wvu.edu/links/adalinks.htm

> A comprehensive site with extensive links to ADA documents and disability-related websites.

Apple Education Disability Resources - http://www.apple.com/accessibility/
> The Worldwide Disability Solutions Group provides technology and learning resources for people with special needs. Also includes a catalog of Apple products and computer software designed to make computers more accessible.

Bobby - http://www.cast.org/bobby/
> This site provide a free service to web page authors by helping them identify and repair significant barriers to access by individuals with disabilities.

Closing the Gap - http://closingthegap.com/
> Closing the Gap, Inc. is an organization that focuses on computer technology for people with special needs through its bi-monthly newspaper, annual international conference and extensive web site.

College Board – <u>www.collegeboard.com</u>
> A not-for-profit membership organization whose mission is to connect students to college success and opportunity. The College Board provides programs and services in college admissions, guidance, assessment, financial aid, enrollment, and teaching and learning. Among its best-known programs are the SAT, the PSAT/NMSQT, and the Advanced Placement Program (AP).

Cornucopia of Disability Information - <u>http://codi.buffalo.edu/</u>
> A comprehensive collection of links to disability web sites.

Disability Rights Education and Defense Fund (DREDF) -
> <u>http://bapd.org/gdiand-1.html</u>
> DREDF advocates at local, state, and national levels through policy reform, legal representation, and education.

Family Village - http://www.familyvillage.wisc.edu/

    A global community that integrates information and resources and provides communication opportunities on the Internet for people with mental retardation and other disabilities, as well as their families and those who provide services and support. Offers informational resources on specific diagnoses, communication connections, adaptive products and technology, adaptive recreational activities, education, worship, health issues, disability-related media, literature and more.

IBM Accessibility Center - http://www-3.ibm.com/able/

    Uses technology as a way to enhance the employability, education, and quality of life of people who have disabilities. Also includes information about assistive devices developed by IBM in order to make software and computers more accessible and user friendly.

International Disability News Ticker - http://www.abilityinfo.com/ticker.html
> This site provides up-to-date news reports about issues related to all types of disabilities. These reports are divided into three searchable areas of interest.

Job Accommodation Network - http://www.jan.wvu.edu/
> The Job Accommodation Network (JAN) is not a job placement service, but an international consulting service that provides information about job accommodations and the employability of people with disabilities. JAN is a free service that provides information on how to accommodate specific functional limitations, with a database of more than 16,000 specific accommodations.

Legal and Advocacy Resources - http://www.makoa.org/legal.htm
> An extensive list of links, legal issues and advocacy concerning disability-related issues.

Microsoft Accessibility - http://www.microsoft.com/enable
> A catalog of innovative products designed to make computers accessible to all.

National Center for Disability Services - http://www.ncds.org
> A center dedicated to the advancement of people with disabilities. Works to create environments that are inclusive of all people.

National Center on Educational Outcomes -
> http://www.education.umn.edu/NCEO
> The NCEO provides national leadership in the identification of outcomes and indicators to monitor educational results for all students, including students with disabilities. Specific topics include the participation of students with disabilities in national and state assessments, standard-setting efforts and graduation requirements.

National Information Center for Children and Youth with Disabilities (NICHCY) - http://www.nichcy.org/
>   NICHCY is a national information and referral center that provides information on disabilities and disability-related issues for families, educators, and other professionals focusing on children and youth, birth to age 22.

National Rehabilitation Information Center (NARIC) - http://www.naric.com
>   Complete literature collection, including commercially published books, journal articles, and audiovisuals - averages about 200 new documents per month. Serves anyone, professional or lay person, who is interested in disability and rehabilitation, including consumers, family members, health professionals, educators, rehabilitation counselors, students, librarians, administrators and researchers.

Regional Disability & Business Technical Assistance Centers (DBTAC's) - request your region's website by calling (800) 949-4232

> Regional offices provide individuals, businesses and government entities with information, materials and technical assistance regarding the Americans with Disabilities Act (ADA).

RESNA Technical Assistance Project Policy Information Pipeline - http://www.resna.org/taproject/about/index.html

> Provides resources and assistance in all major policy areas including community living, education, employment, health care, telecommunications and information technology.

WebAble - http://www.webable.com/

> This site is dedicated to making the Internet accessible to people with disabilities. Extensive information is provided on accessibility software.

Yahoo! Society and Culture, Disability -
    http://dir.yahoo.com/society_and_culture/disabilities

* *Portions excerpted from* Web Resources for Assisting College Students with Disabilities *by Roger O. Smith, Jill Warnke & Dave Edyburn of the University of Wisconsin-Milwaukee and Noelle K. Kurth & Daryl F. Mellard of the University of Kansas. Compilation of this website list was supported in whole or in part by the US Department of Education, Office of Special Education Programs, (Cooperative Agreement No. H324M980109). Reprinted with permission.*

Students Speak Out

Be as self-sufficient as possible. Take advantage of the services, but don't count on them to do everything for you.

It's gotta be a two-way street. You only get out of your college education what you put into it.

Take some initiative—Stay involved in the process.

Be grateful. Thank the people who help you.

Keep a positive attitude.

I view the benefits I receive as a privilege, not a right. Don't abuse it.

Get to know your professors. Let them know what your situation is and establish a rapport. As a matter of fact, establish a rapport with everyone you can, including fellow students. It will make your life a lot easier.

I wish I knew how to study right. I really wasn't prepared for what I need to learn in college.

Study groups with other students help a lot. Use them, or get one going yourself.

I wish I had had a little less fun and studied more.

Oh man, could I have used a planner! If I knew how important it could be to keep me focused a little earlier, I maybe wouldn't be on academic probation now.

I wish I had gotten more involved in student groups from the beginning.

I didn't do my homework about services available to me. If I had known what all was available, I think I could've been more successful.

I wish I had known that people are really accepting so I wouldn't have been so afraid to get into a new situation.

People have turned out to be great! I was a little embarrassed to meet new people, but you just need to jump in and do it. Things can be easier than you think if you just be yourself.

You're pretty much on your own in college. This can be good, but not so good if you're used to having it soft.

I didn't know I wouldn't get the same kinds of breaks I got in high school. I wish I did so I could be more ready for what I need to do now.

Internships help in the long run. After all, the whole goal is to get a good job, right?

You should know if you're a good student or not. If you're only a fair student, things aren't going to get easier in college.

Give yourself enough time so you're not so stressed.

I know I'm smart.—I just never learned how to study. Should've done that before I got here!

Accommodations don't take the place of knowing what you need to for a test. You don't know it, you're going to flunk—disability or no disability.

Make sure to get enough skills in high school so it doesn't shock you when you get to college.

Get involved, get a job, join a club, whatever.

Don't mess around. Get with the program early and have a goal.

It's tough being older than most students, and even more so because I wasn't disabled before. So I've got a lot of new stuff to deal with.

I just want to fit in; but sometimes I need to make arrangements to do it.

People get freaked out when they realize I can't hear. It's not such a big deal. You can write a note if you need to.

If your reading level isn't so great, you should consider how you're going to understand your textbooks.

Reading all the books is tough for me.

Computers are everywhere! You better learn how to use them if you're going to make it.

I discovered people make friends with me because of who I am as a person.—Not because I have an obvious disability.

You can't just complain and give up. Learn how to work through the problems and be willing to help come up with solutions. I almost gave up, but I'm glad I didn't. I'm graduating in the spring!

I wish I knew about how the voc. rehab. agency could help me with my education before I got here. I'm glad I know now!

Don't be afraid to get help from your professors. Explain what you need. Sometimes they just don't know [how to help].

Index by Item Number

O

Office for Civil Rights (OCR) #45
Otherwise Qualified #27
Orientation #7, 8
Orientation and Mobility Training #8

P

Pass Fail Option #72
Paths of Travel #61
Personal Care Attendants #40, 78
Personal Services #40
Personal Statement #6
Preference #4,10
Placement Tests #8

Priority Registration #58
Psychiatric Disability #22
Psychiatric Services #13

R

Reading Comprehension #51
Real Time Captioning #62
Reasonable Accommodations #48
Recording for the Blind and Dyslexic #36
Reader #37
Read Please #36
Rehabilitation Act of 1973 #11
Roommates #76, 77, 78

S

T

Reviewer Comments

Trudie Hines and Kendra Johnson have co-authored a terrific resource that will help students with disabilities appreciate the significant transition they are likely to undergo if they are entering college for the first time. Their tips and practical advice, especially if considered and implemented before beginning college, will help prepare the student to successfully transition to higher learning. Sadly, unrealistic expectations occasioned by lack of understanding between special education services and reasonable accommodations has resulted in some students, who truly possess the talents and abilities to be successful, to experience difficulties that in some cases could have been avoided. Finally, a book written expressly for the student rather than the parents, should go a long way in bridging the knowledge gap and enable the student to have a positive experience. Written in a positive – yet realistic tone, *100 Things Every College Student With a Disability Ought to Know* makes the perfect graduation present: from middle school. I encourage guidance counselors and transition specialists to read this valuable book and make it available to all their college-bound students with disabilities.

—*Jeanne Kincaid*

Jeanne M. Kincaid, Esq., is a Shareholder in the law firm of Bernstein, Shur, Sawyer & Nelson and a member of its Advanced Educational Solutions practice group, and a noted authority on the Americans with Disabilities Act and the Individuals with Disabilities Education Act.

My colleagues Trudie Hines and Kendra Johnson have done a great job in writing *100 Things Every College Student With a Disability Ought to Know*. Their many years of experience serving countless students with disabilities is clearly evidenced in the advice they give. Students who read this book and follow the advice in it are far less likely to experience a disastrous college experience compared to less well prepared students.

Trudie and Kendra's advice is applicable to students attending Community Colleges, Technical Colleges or Ivy League Universities. It applies to undergraduate, graduate and professional schools. It is "must reading" whether you are picking the first university you will attend or looking to transfer.

This book is clearly written and avoids much of the legal jargon associated with postsecondary disability support services. Furthermore, it is written assuming the prospective college student as the reader and not their parents. This foreshadows what will happen when the student enrolls at a college or university.

—*Sam Goodin*

Past President of the Association on Higher Education and Disability

Director, University of Michigan Office of Services for Students with Disabilities

---

100 Things Every College Student With a Disability Ought to Know is an excellent resource for students with disabilities. This book answers general questions many students have regardless of their disability or type of institution of higher learning they are attending. Students with knowledge from this book will have a "head start" on transitioning to institutes of higher learning. I would recommend students and their parents read *100 Things Every College Student With a Disability Ought to Know* before they attend their preferred institution of higher learning. This knowledge will allow them to ask more in-depth questions about the services they can expect from the Office of Disability Services at their institution of choice. This is a must read book for students with disabilities.

—*Paul Nolting, Ph.D.*

Paul D. Nolting, Ph.D., is president of Academic Success Press, Inc. and author of the Mathematic Learning Disability Handbook and Winning at Math. He is a noted expert in learning disabilities.

I was so pleased to have been asked to review *100 Things Every College Student With a Disability Ought to Know*. I have always felt that there needed to be a publication to help bridge the gap for students with disabilities between high school and college. Starting college can be an overwhelming experience for any student. However, without adequate preparation, students with disabilities are more likely to run into problems early on that can escalate into more serious matters later. This life changing transition requires much advance thinking and in addition to the issues that other students face- like time management, money management, eating properly, and health issues- students with disabilities also have to learn very quickly how to arrange for a multitude of services- including how to use accommodations, ensuring that their housing arrangements will fit their needs and that their materials are available in alternative formats in time for their use. This book has taken some of the craziness of the maze out of the process for students with disabilities. I would strongly encourage any student with a disability who will be starting college in the next year to read this book before they get to campus so that they know what is expected of them, what the institution is responsible for and what they need to do to navigate the system so that they will then know all that they need in order to have equal access to their education. Welcome to college!

—*Emily K. Singer*
Director, Disability Services
University of Tennessee

The combined experiences of Kendra Johnson and Trudie Hines in providing access for students with disabilities in postsecondary education have resulted in this valuable guide for students with disabilities.

100 Things Every College Student With a Disability Ought to Know is unique in that its focus is the student! The book not only provides students with disabilities with information on successful navigation of postsecondary cultures but, maybe more importantly, it makes students realize that they must take responsibility for their disability.

I would recommend that this book be read by any student with a disability who is thinking of attending any college or professional training school at the time when they start to explore the possibilities beyond secondary education.

100 Things Every College Student With a Disability Ought to Know is a definite guide to success!

—*Duraese' Hall*, DSS Coordinator
University of Houston-Downtown
AHEAD member since 1990

Student Reviews

I wish I had had access to this book during my senior year in high school! This book was very well researched, and any student with a disability should have this book in their possession. This book gives a real representation of what students planning on going to college should expect out of their disability services office. Great job on presenting real life situations and scenarios for students with disabilities!

—*Kelly Snyder*, Junior, Communication Major

100 Things Every College Student With a Disability Ought to Know is a wonderful tool for any student with a disability. Starting college can be a confusing and stressful experience. The information and resources in this book can definitely make the experience much easier. Reading this book will help students with disabilities know what is expected from them in college. It also lets the student know what is expected from the college. Every student with a disability should read and study this book!

—*Jeremy Westover*, Freshman, Early Childhood Education-Special Needs Major

I consider *100 Things Every College Student With a Disability Ought to Know* to be a "must read" for any student with a disability who plans to attend college. The numbered, itemized format was easy to read and understand. The web resources included in this handbook help to inform the student about their rights and a host of other topics. This useful tool should be provided to all students who need accommodations upon entry to any college or university.

Many thanks to Trudie and Kendra for sharing their knowledge with the rest of us!

—*Jackie Mercer*, Sophomore, Social Work Major

While reading this book, all I could think of was, "Boy, do I wish I had an excellent resource like this when I started my college education. It would have made my life so much easier." There is so much here that I wish I had known from the start. Every student with a disability needs this book.

—*Becky Borka*, Junior, Education Major

Credits

Cartoons by Michael F. Giangreco

> From *Teaching Old Logs New Tricks: More Absurdities and Realities of Education* by Michael F. Griangreco © 2000, Peytral Publications, Inc. Reprinted with permission. Cartoon: "Laboratory Retriever"

> From *Flying by the Seat of Your Pants: More Realities and Absurdities of Special Eduacation* by Michael F. Griangreco © 1999, Peytral Publications, Inc. Reprinted with permission. Cartoons: "Appropriate Labels," "New Disability Categories," "Crazy Like a Fox."

Cartoon by John Callahan

> From *Don't Worry: He Won't Get Far by Foot* © by John Callahan. Reprinted with permission. Cartoon: "The Tagger."

About the Publisher
The Cambridge Stratford Study Skills Institute

Cambridge Stratford, Ltd. formed The Cambridge Stratford Study Skills Institute in 1985 with the help of its current president, Peter W. Stevens, a former vice president from a private college in New York. It is an international organization of learning and study skills specialists and tutor training professionals dedicated to helping students of all ages to STUDY SMARTER, READ FASTER and SCORE HIGHER ON TESTS, key ingredients for success in school as well as in life.

Cambridge Stratford Study Skills Course System

The CSSS INSTITUTE provides teacher and tutor training services, private courses for students in summer and after school programs nationally, and publishes the internationally renowned study skills curriculum entitled **The Cambridge Stratford Study Skills Course**. It is taught publicly by schools, colleges, federal and state grant programs at 3 levels (6–8th: 20 hour edition, 9–11th: 30 hour edition, and 12–15th: 10 hour edition, entitled *Ten Tips for Academic Success*, available in English and Spanish). These editions include 4 components; Student Workbook, Teacher Manual, Transparency and Listening Tape Set.

Tutor Training Research Study

In 1994, The INSTITUTE introduced a research-based tutor training curriculum nationally under the direction of Dr. Ross MacDonald entitled *The Master Tutor: A Guidebook for More Effective Tutoring*. It includes the state-of-the-art methods tutors can use to improve one-on-one tutoring sessions and consists of a self-instructional Guidebook for tutors, a Tutor Trainer's Manual, and Transparency Set. A pre- and post-assessment, **The TESAT** (Tutor Evaluation and Self-Assessment Tool) is available for validating improved tutoring skills.

Starting 2002-2003, the *Online eMaster Tutor Training Course* was introduced to assist tutor trainers in training peer and staff tutors online. A train-the-trainer course, the *Online eMaster Tutor Trainer's Course*, was also made available to train online instructors in effectively teaching tutors using a hybrid of face-to-face and online instructional components.

Improving the Retention of College Students

The CSSS INSTITUTE's mission is to help students prepare for and succeed in college. In addition to this newest book for college students with a disability, four other self-orientation to college books have been published to help traditional, non-traditional adult college-bound students, online learners, and international students adjust to the difficult transitions required in becoming a successful college student. These navigation-to-college guidebooks, ***100 Things Every Freshman Ought to Know***, ***100 Things Every Adult College Student Ought to Know***, ***100 Things Every Online Student Ought to Know***, and ***100 Things Every International Student Ought to Know*** are suggested reading for all those starting college for the first time as well as those who may be returning to college after a lapse in time. Pre college and college preparation programs may find them helpful in building college persistence and retention among their students since each assists students in understanding college customs, practices, vocabulary, and procedures, plus each includes important tips for balancing responsibilities in college, family, and work environments.

NOTE: Prospective Authors — The *100 Things* series can be expanded to help others. If you have an idea, book, or concept that might help students succeed in school or college, please contact us at the address on the next page or via e-mail. We're interested!

If you need information about any of the products or services offered or would like a sample lesson (PREVIEW MANUAL) forwarded for your review, write or call today.

The Cambridge Stratford Study Skills Institute
8560 Main Street
Williamsville, New York 14221
(716) 626-9044 or FAX (716) 626-9076
Cambridges@aol.com
http://www.cambridgestratford.com

This book is made available in alternative format upon request.